Hope

A Daily Devotional

Hope

A Daily Devotional

Julie Bernard
With
Emily Dempster
Joanne Mueller
Becky Griffiths

What are you seeking that no other relationship has satisfied? Are you looking for hope in relationships, jobs, money, health and material things? Are you trying to find healing, safety, peace, or guidance? Do you desire a friend who is always there and never lets you down? Whatever your need, your hope is in the Living God. Hope is a confident expectation of a guaranteed result.

To have hope in God requires knowing who He is. Unfortunately, many of us have a very skewed view of who God actually is. We decide who God is based on our past, our circumstances, our feelings, or our desire of who God needs to be instead of looking to God's Word for who God says He is. Such knowledge from God's Word of our Maker's identity is the essence of eternal life: "This is eternal life, that they may know You, the only true God, and Jesus Christ whom You have sent" (John 17:3). It's not enough that God knows us; He wants us to know Him. Possessing this knowledge of Him yields a life with meaning, life with eternal significance, and a place to put our hope.

Scripture promises that if we seek Him, we will find Him. God wants to be found. Since Genesis 1:1, God has been revealing Himself to man through His various names, attributes, characteristics and promises each revealing who He is, why we should trust Him, why we so desperately need Him, and why we can only put our hope in Him.

He is our hope,

Julie Bernard

DAY 1 | Hope in God Who is Almighty

Psalm 91:1-2

"He who dwells in the shelter of the Most High will rest in the shadow of the Almighty. I will say of the Lord, 'He is my refuge and my fortress, my God, in whom I trust.'"

⚓ Sometimes life seems out of control, overwhelming even. It is easy to forget that God is Almighty! No circumstance is too complicated or difficult for Him. We can have confident assurance that He is mighty enough to always protect, and to always provide. He will always be trustworthy and will always keep His promises. He is our Almighty God!

While Marcie threw a fifth load of laundry in the wash, she bounced Sadie on her hip. The others kiddos were in bed and dreams of a quiet moment alone had been dashed earlier when Sadie had fallen asleep in the car. Sadie was now wide awake. Being up late the night before talking with her husband about what God had laid on their hearts to do and the impossibility of their situation left her exhausted. With hardly any time to process the things they had talked about with children to care for and a household to manage, Marcie felt bombarded from all sides, drowning almost. She desperately wanted to have answers to the questions swirling in her head.

Yet, she had hope! She knew that there was One who wasn't drowning and didn't feel the pressure of the never-ending days. She knew that the same God who declared "I am God Almighty" to Abram was the same God who declared to her, "I am God Almighty!" She could count on His promises, His protection, and His timing in working out the things on her mind and heart. She sighed as she closed the washer lid. She gave Sadie a kiss, grabbed Sadie's blankie and book, and snuggled into the overstuffed chair in the living room, placing her burden at His feet.

The first time God declares Himself El Shaddai, God Almighty, covenant-keeper, protector, and provider, is in Genesis 17. Like

Marcie, Abram was also in the midst of never-ending tasks and days. The routine of the seasons, of managing his household, and the pressure of producing an heir was all pressing in. God had promised Abram an heir from his own body. *How many more days, months, years, would he have to defend this God to the lack he and his wife Sarai felt?* He worked year after year to build an inheritance but had no son to pass it on to. Genesis 37:1-2 states, "Now when Abram was ninety-nine years old, the Lord appeared to Abram and said to him, 'I am God Almighty; walk before me and be blameless. I will establish my covenant between me and you, and I will multiply you exceedingly.'" God declared His name and nature. He declared that His words did mean something. He declared that He had not forgotten but would confirm the things He'd said before. In the passage following this declaration, God promises that Abram would be the father of many nations, that kings would come from his line, that the covenant God initiated and established would be everlasting, and that it would be between God, Abram, and Abram's descendants. He promised land, protection, and blessing. God promised that the heir He would provide would come from Abram and his wife, Sarai.

God Almighty. He is powerful protector, covenant keeper, and the God who blesses those under His protection. God makes covenants with divine knowledge and understanding and with the power to see them come into fruition. For those of us on the other side of the cross, we know that God has fulfilled much of what He promised to Abraham and that much more is to come. We also know that those of us who are Abraham's children, through faith, are heirs of that covenant. We can have confident assurance of a guaranteed result because we can be confident in who God has proclaimed Himself to be, God Almighty!

How does knowing that God declares of Himself, "I am God Almighty," provide hope for you today?

Praise Him for being God Almighty.

For further study read Genesis 17 and Psalm 91.

DAY 2

Hope in God My Deliverer

2 Samuel 22:1-3

"And David spoke the words of this song to the LORD in the day that the LORD delivered him from the hand of all his enemies and from the hand of Saul. He said, 'The LORD is my rock and my fortress and my deliverer; My God, my rock, in whom I take refuge, My shield and the horn of my salvation, my stronghold and my refuge; My savior, You save me from violence.'"

Victory is what we long for. We struggle, we suffer, and we wonder how our circumstances will turn out. From children who are ill to unemployment to aging parents, we ache and long for deliverance. Sometimes our suffering is a result of our own sin, sometimes the sin of another. If it is a result of our own sin, layered on top of the longing is our guilt. Either way, we have hope, confident assurance, in God our deliverer.

In 2 Samuel 21, David fought Israel's long-time enemy the Philistines. The fighting was so intense and lasted so long, that he became weary (v. 15). David's life had been in peril! Despite David's many enemies God delivered David, even providing victory over his powerful enemies. David knew that it was not he, nor his men, who defeated the Philistines. It was God, his deliverer.

In the midst of the battle, David knew where to go for victory. "I call upon the LORD, who is worthy to be praised, and I am saved from my enemies. In my distress I called upon the LORD; to my God I called. From his temple he heard my voice, and my cry came to his ears." (2 Samuel 22:4,7) David had a pattern of going to God when in trouble. After the battle, David praised God, his deliverer. "He said, The LORD is my rock and my fortress and my deliverer." (2 Samuel 22:2) The victory belonged to God.

We need a deliverer in our lives. God's character never changes, and the same God who delivered David, is our deliverer. Our greatest need for deliverance is from the chains of our own sin. Our sin nature prevents us from having fellowship and eternal life with God. Sin has a price, and that price is too much for us to pay. Paul wrote in Romans 6:23, "For the wages is the sin is death, but the free gift of God is eternal life in Christ Jesus our Lord." God loves us so much that He paid the price for our sin when He sent Jesus to earth. Jesus came as a man to earth, died on the cross, rose from the grave on the third day, and ascended back in heaven where He is alive and seated at the right hand of God. Jesus, God the son, is our great deliverer. Paul tells us in Romans 10, "that if you confess with your mouth Jesus as Lord, and believe in your heart that God raised Him from the dead, you will be saved."

I need God to help me and deliver me when I face difficult circumstances, but my greatest need is for Him to deliver me from not only the price of sin which is death, but also the power of sin in my everyday life. Every day I struggle with sin, however, I can ask God to help me not sin and rather live and think the way He wants me to. Often I fail, but God, my deliverer, forgives me readily when I confess my sin. Because of all God has done and continues to do, I live delivered and free.

Why has God delivered us at such and exorbitant price, the cost of His Son? David explains in 2 Samuel 22:20, "He brought me out into a broad place: he rescued me, because he delighted in me." He delights in us. Will you seek God, your deliverer, today?

How does knowing God is your deliverer provide hope for you today?

Praise Him for being your deliverer.

For further study, read 2 Samuel 22 and Psalm 40.

DAY 3

Hope in God My Provider

Psalm 145:16

"You open your hand and satisfy the desire of every living thing."

Safety, food, water, clothes, comfort, relationship. So often our thoughts go to our physical, emotional, and spiritual needs, and how we might fill these needs. Unless we depend on God's promise that He understands our needs and will provide, we are tempted to be overwhelmed, to worry, or even to put our confidence in ourselves and our own solutions. However, when we recognize that God is the one who is our provider, that He even delights in providing for us, we can have confident assurance that He will provide, and at just the right time!

Stories of God's provision are all around us! In our own community, there is a women's shelter that experiences God's timely provision multiple times per week. This summer I heard an account from the kitchen supervisor of God's timely provision. Recently, while working in the kitchen preparing a taco salad, she noticed that there wasn't any tortilla chips or tortillas and simply said, "Lord, it would be so nice to have some tortillas to go with this meal." Not two minutes later the delivery bell sounded. It was a local church delivering surplus from their own food closet. Included in the donation were several packages of tortillas! What a timely donation! God had provided in advance for the need she had just recognized. Tortillas weren't necessary, but it confirmed again to this woman how God sees and knows and takes special care of His children. Any father or mother delights in meeting the needs of their children in ways that are personal and timely. God is our perfect Father and provider. This woman rejoiced, and continually rejoices, at the ways God shows that He is a perfect provider.

God sees ALL of our needs. He sees our physical, emotional, and spiritual needs. Provider. Provision. Pro-vision. God is our perfect provider even before we know we have a problem or a need for a solution.

Romans 5:8 speaks of our deepest need and God's most important provision, "But God demonstrates His own love toward us, in that while we were yet sinners, Christ died for us." God provided salvation out of love for us before we even knew we needed a Savior, before we knew we were dirty with sin. This is God's greatest act of pro-vision for us, and Jesus perfectly provided for us by giving His life for ours. When we stop and dwell on God's provision of salvation, what hope it gives!

Hope, not only for our future, but for every day between now and when we see our Savior face to face. He continues and will continue His good work in us until our last day here on earth. (Philippians 1:6)

In addition to our spiritual needs, in Matthew 6, Jesus gives us a beautiful picture of His thoughts towards our physical needs, His provision for His creation, and His desire for the focus of our attention. Jesus commands that we are not to be anxious about our physical needs, consumed with making money, or priding ourselves in providing for ourselves. He feeds the birds of the air and clothes the lilies of the field beautifully and bountifully. "Are you not much more valuable than they," Jesus asks? "Your heavenly Father knows that you need them. But seek first His kingdom and His righteousness, and all these things will be given to you as well. (Matthew 6: 32b-33). We can have hope, a confident assurance, in God as our perfect provider for all of our needs.

How does knowing God is our provider, give you hope for today?

Praise Him for being your provider.

For further study, read Matt 6:25-33, and Philippians 4:6-7, 19

DAY 4

Hope in God Who is Faithful

Deuteronomy 7:9

"Know therefore that the LORD your God, He is God, the faithful God, who keeps His covenant and His lovingkindness to a thousandth generation with those who love Him and keep His commands;"

"Know therefore that the LORD your God, He is God, the faithful God." It is who He is; we know His character is unchanging (Hebrews 13:8). We are people who long for those around us to be faithful. How often though, do we fail? We fail all the time. Yet, God never fails. He is faithful. We can have confident assurance in God's faithfulness. We can be secure children and have peace in any circumstance because our God is faithful. He is faithfully present, and He faithfully carries out His promises to us.

A beautiful example of God's faithfulness is the account of Joseph. Joseph, the son of Jacob, the son of Isaac, the son of Abraham, was number 11 in a long line of brothers. He was daddy's favorite. Because of the obvious favoritism, Joseph's brothers hated him. They were jealous. This jealousy led to a very tragic event in Joseph's life. Joseph's brothers sold him into slavery. Think about that for a moment; one moment he was the favored son of a very, very wealthy man, and the next he was on his way to a faraway country destined to be a slave to who knows who, doing who knows what. In Genesis 39:2 we see a statement. This statement breathes of something so far greater than anyone can imagine. "The Lord was with Joseph and he prospered." Because of the Lord's presence, because of His faithfulness, Joseph found favor in the eyes of his Egyptian master. As we read, we see that Joseph's hardship was far from over. Joseph was thrown into jail because of a false accusation. But again, because of God's presence, Joseph found favor in the eyes of the head jailer and was put into a position of leadership.

Fast forward some time later, we find Joseph second-in-command to Pharaoh himself. In this position, he was not only able to save his family from starvation but also helped millions of others live through a great famine.

Listen in on this conversation; Joseph's faith and hope was in a faithful God. Here he is speaking to his brothers when finally his identity is revealed to them after many long years apart.

"Now do not be grieved or angry with yourselves, because you sold me here, for God sent me before you to preserve life. For the famine *has been* in the land these two years, and there are still five years in which there will be neither plowing nor harvesting. God sent me before you to preserve for you a remnant in the earth, and to keep you alive by a great deliverance. Now, therefore, it was not you who sent me here, but God; and He has made me a father to Pharaoh and lord of all his household and ruler over all the land of Egypt." Genesis 45:5-8

The dictionary says that faithful means: Steadfast, dedicated, dependable, and worthy of trust. God certainly is steadfast. He doesn't waver. He doesn't second-guess. God certainly is dedicated. He is dedicated to see his own purposes carried out for our good. And God is certainly dependable and worthy of trust. God's word is a testimony of His faithfulness. As His children we can have confident assurance that our God is a faithful.

Hebrews 10:23 "Let us hold fast to the confession of our hope without wavering, for He who promised is faithful".

How does knowing God is faithful provide hope for you today?

Praise Him for being faithful to you.

For further study read Genesis 37, 39-45

DAY 5 | Hope in God Who is Lord and Master

Isaiah 6:1

"In the year of King Uzziah's death I saw the Lord sitting on the throne, lofty and exalted, with the train of His robe filling the temple."

Early in our marriage, we had the opportunity to move to Reno, Nevada, for a job opportunity for my husband. We finally decided to go, but that evening I felt sick about the decision. Sometimes we don't know what to do next in our lives. We find ourselves either unsure of which direction to take, or we strongly desire to go our own way. We can have hope, confident assurance, that our God ordained the number of our days before we were ever created (Psalm 139:16), that God, our Lord and Master, has a plan for our lives (Jeremiah 29:11), and that He has good work for us to do (Ephesians 2:10).

Isaiah states in Isaiah chapter 6 that in the year of King Uzziah's death, he saw the Lord on His throne exalted. Seraphim stood above the Lord in Isaiah's vision and called out to one another declaring God's holiness. The foundations of the thresholds trembled at their voices and the temple was filled with smoke. His vision reveals God's identity as our sovereign Lord and Master who is lifted up on high.

In response to seeing God in His glory, Isaiah was deeply aware of his sin. In verse 5, he said, "Woe is me, for I am ruined!" When confronted with God's holiness, we become aware of our own sin as well. We are cleansed of our sin through Christ's blood shed on the cross. In Isaiah's vision, one of the seraphim flew to him with a burning coal and touched his lips and stated that he was forgiven. Isaiah's vision didn't end here, though.

"Then I heard the voice of the Lord, saying, 'Whom shall I send, and who will go for US?' Then I said, "Here am I.

Send me!'" (Isaiah 6:8) After being cleansed of his sin, Isaiah responded to God, his Lord and Master, and was willing to go wherever God sent him. He was ready and willing to obey God in whatever God asked of him. His heart was full of gratitude and submission, and his view of God was correct. God was mighty, exalted, and was seated on the throne above all. Are we willing to go where ever God sends us? Will we pray and seek God's direction in our own lives? Is our view of God correct?

We have hope, confident assurance, that our God, who is Lord and Master, knows the details of whatever circumstances we are in today. He has a plan. Jeremiah 29:11 states, "'For I know the plans that I have for you,' declares the Lord, 'plans for welfare and not for calamity to give you a future and a hope.'" That plan includes the good work of making us more like Jesus as well as the good work He planned ahead of time for us to participate in. Paul writes to the church at Ephesus in Ephesians 2:10, "For we are His workmanship, created in Christ Jesus for good works, which God prepared beforehand so that we would walk in them." God's plan for each one of us is intentional and specific.

We ended up deciding to stay in Oregon and didn't move to Reno. After praying about it, we did not have peace about going. God, our Lord and Master, had good works here for us to do. Like Isaiah, we were willing to do whatever it was He asked of us. He wants us to trust Him, and He wants us to be willing to follow Him where ever He sends us. Our hope rests in our God who is Lord and Master and His good plan.

How does knowing God is Lord and Master provide hope for you today?

Praise Him for being Lord and Master.

For further study, read Psalm 139.

DAY 6

Hope in God Who is My Father

Galatians 4:6

"Because you are sons, God has sent for the
Spirit of His Son into our hearts,
crying "Abba! Father!"

When one speaks of her father, either warm memories are generated, or stories flow from hurting hearts. And there are those like Cleo, who never knew her father. All she remembered was that he had a rather warm smile, and she thought he liked to sing. *"But, was that true,"* she wondered? Or, was that what she imagined about the man in the picture she still carried? He had left her, her mother, and two older siblings when she was only three.

Our earthly father paints the first picture we see of our Heavenly Father. Sadly, because we are all sinners, that picture can be severely distorted. Thankfully, God's portrait is illustrated throughout all of Scripture so that we can see, know, and have a relationship with the living God, our forever Father!

Our forever Father is perfect in all of His ways (Matthew 5:48). Nothing will ever separate us from His love (Romans 8:39).

Let that truth soak in! You have a faithful, loving, just, and holy Father. A Father who is perfect in all His ways; He is perfect in everything He does with you. He will never leave you or abandon you. He will loving correct you, and direct you. He is always available to you, never too busy, never preoccupied, never harsh, or impatient.

Your forever Father has adopted you to be His very own. He choose you! He snatched you straight out of darkness, helplessness, and destruction. He saved you from a life void of hope.

Are you wandering aimlessly? Your forever Father will lead you, just as a faithful father takes his young daughter's hand as they cross the busy street together, He will direct your steps. Are you fearful of the future? Your forever Father has a plan all mapped out for you. He will care for you and see you through each step of the journey. He will be your counselor, providing wisdom through His Word and His Spirit. He will catch you every time you leap out in faith.

Is your heart hurting as a result of circumstances out of your control? Lean into your forever Father. He is your strong tower. He stands with you.

Are you carrying the weight of sin? Has guilt led you into isolation? Your forever Father offers complete forgiveness. His loving, strong arms are wide open, longing to welcome you back home.

Are you smack dab in the middle of a trial? Your forever Father is using it for your good. He will take the difficulty and refine you and help you to look more like His Son, Jesus! He deeply desires for you to share in the family resemblance.
Are you fearful? Your forever Father holds you close, protecting and providing for you!

It was God's love that prompted Him to make us His forever children (Ephesians 1:5). We didn't choose Him, He choose us. We are absolutely secure. He will never give up on us, or leave us. We will always have our forever Father! He is our perfect Father that we can know, love and trust. A Father that welcomes us, cherishes us, provides for us, and tenderly leads us.

What hope we have because God is our forever Father. We can confidently expect that He will always treat us like His cherished children, because that is who we are!

How does knowing God is your Father provide hope for you today?

Praise Him for being your forever Father.

For further study read I Peter 1:1-10

DAY 7

Hope In the Lord My Righteousness

2 Corinthians 5:21

"He made Him who knew no sin to be sin on our behalf, so that we might become the righteousness of God in Him."

Samantha appeared much older than her age; it was obvious life had dealt its blows. She lived alone with no friends to speak of, and she no longer had any relationship with her son or daughter. Life was empty, cruel, and held no hope.

Although suffering from several mini strokes, Virginia had a twinkle in her eye and her smile lit up her hospital room. She spoke of Jesus and His care for her, and the hope that she had because of Him. The contrast between these two women couldn't be ignored.

What was the difference? Had one worked harder? Had one just lived a more fortunate life? In His Word, God levels the playing field. In Romans 3, He tells us that every single one of us have sinned. There is not one of us who is righteous. All of us have rebelled against God. We all have gone our own way and have countless times sinned against God. Consequently every single one of us are deserving of and destined for eternal punishment and separation from God. Apart from Christ, we are all hopeless, that includes Samantha, Virginia, and everyone in between.

The tribe of Judah was no exception. They refused to obey God and had no interest in spiritual things. Left to themselves they were in a state of moral decay and sin ran rampant. Despite their sin, God promised in Jeremiah 23:5-7 that He would send a Savior, and His name would be "The Lord Our Righteousness". What hope!

The tribe of Judah could never be good enough; Samantha and Virgina could never be good enough. We can never be good enough, nor can we work hard enough to satisfy God's standard of perfection on our own. Praise God we don't have to!

Christ made the great exchange on our behalf. 2 Corinthians 5:21 explains that Christ being perfect and without sin took our sin and gave us His righteousness. The very moment we put our faith in Jesus, He forgives us of all our sins, past, present and future. He also frees us from slavery to any and all sins. He has declared us innocent of our sins and pronounced us righteous with the very righteousness of Jesus.

Since Jesus is our righteousness, we can rest in knowing God has only love for us and our relationship is secure. When we do sin, God isn't mad, He doesn't disregard us, He doesn't turn a cold shoulder to us, He just longs for us to repent and confess our sins to Him. He willingly and lovingly forgives. (Luke 15).

Since Jesus is our righteousness we don't have to keep on sinning. We no longer are we who we once were. We are no longer dominated by sin, now we are alive to Christ. (Romans 6).

Since Jesus is our righteousness, we are no longer chained to guilt or regret! Instead, we are free to live out our free gift of salvation, to live out the righteousness that has been given to us through Christ. When Jesus is our righteousness, there is never a day that we have to live plagued by sin, fearful of our future or sabotaged by guilt! (Psalm 103:12).

Jesus makes all the difference! "He rescued us from the domain of darkness, and transferred us to the kingdom of His beloved Son, in whom we have redemption, the forgiveness of sins." (Colossians 1:13-14). We can always have hope, confident expectation, in Christ. Our relationship with the Lord is secure, and our future with Him is sure because He is our righteousness!

How does knowing God is your righteousness give you hope today?

Praise Him for being your righteousness.

For further study read Isaiah 53.

DAY 8

Hope in God Who is my Shepherd

Psalm 23:1-3a

"The Lord is my Shepherd, I shall not want. He makes me lie down in green pastures, He leads me beside quiet waters, He restores my soul;"

We live in a very go, go, go culture. We are always on the move, always being entertained, always looking to the next thing. Messages from the world bombard us while the enemy and our flesh distract us from keeping our eyes fixed on our Shepherd. In the middle of it all, Jesus calls Himself the Great Shepherd (John 10). When we listen and surrender ourselves to the care and protection of Jesus, our Shepherd, we can have confident assurance in His compassionate protection, care, and leading.

Isaiah 53:6 perfectly describes our human state, "All of us like sheep have gone astray, each of us has turned to his own way." It's known that when faced with danger, hunger, and thirst a sheep might wander. They go their own way to try and escape these dangers and satisfy these needs on their own. Instead of staying under the care and leadership of their shepherd, they venture off into dangerous situations without the protection of the shepherd and the fellowship of the herd. Can you relate? Oh, but we have such a loving Shepherd. In Mark 6 we hear that Jesus felt great compassion toward the people He encountered while He was on earth because they were like sheep without a shepherd.

Looking both at Isaiah 53 and John 10 we see just how far the Shepherd went to secure our safety and sonship. Isaiah 53:6 finishes with, "But the Lord has caused the iniquity of us all to fall on Him." John 10:11 says that the good Shepherd lays down His life for His sheep. Jesus did lay down His life, and because of what He accomplished on the cross, those of us who believe in Him are able look to Jesus as our Shepherd. We rely on Him for guidance, teaching, and care. Praise Him, our good Shepherd!

King David knew well the heart of a shepherd. As a young man, he spent his days herding sheep. He lovingly cared for the needs of His sheep. He understood the heart of the shepherd toward his sheep, and the heart of God toward us.

Hear God's heart of compassion, care, and provision in these beautiful words and notice the truth about our Shepherd written by David in Psalm 23.

"The Lord is my Shepherd, I shall not want. He makes me lie down in green pastures; He leads me besides quiet waters. He restores my soul; He guides me in the paths of righteousness for His name's sake. Even though I walk through the valley of the shadow of death, I fear no evil, for You are with me; Your rod and Your staff, they comfort me. You prepare a table before me in the presence of my enemies; You have anointed my head with oil; My cup overflows. Surely goodness and lovingkindness will follow me all the days of my life, and I will dwell in the house of the Lord forever."

So, what do we know about our Shepherd? We know that He has great compassion for us, His sheep. We know this because He laid down His life for us. We also know that His intentions toward us are to provide rest, peace, and restoration of our souls as well as comfort, protection, joy, and such love that we can hardly grasp. The heart of our Shepherd toward us is truly amazing.

Because we have the Good Shepherd, we can be confidently assured of His guidance, protection, and love.

How does knowing that God is your Shepherd provide hope for you today?

Praise Him for being your Shepherd.

For further study, read John 10:11-18

DAY 9

Hope in God Who is Sovereign

Psalm 103:19

"The LORD has established His throne in the heavens, And His sovereignty rules over all."

⚓ After wrestling with knee pain from a torn medial meniscus, my daughter is scheduled for knee surgery in five days. My heart aches from watching her struggle for the past ten weeks, and I am fatigued from helping her manage her pain daily. All of this appears to be without purpose. We are sidelined from other, seemingly more meaningful, activities while we navigate this trial. Life has become a period of painful waiting.

David wrote in Psalm 103:19 that, "His sovereignty rules over all." God's sovereignty rules over our pain and suffering as well as our joys and triumphs. Our circumstances pass through His hands and are allowed into our lives. There is nothing, including pain and suffering, that happens that He does not allow. My daughter's torn meniscus was allowed by our sovereign God, and it is being used by Him for our good.

In Romans 8:28, the apostle Paul wrote, "And we know that God causes all things to work together for good to those who love God, to those who are called according to His purpose." We may feel that we are missing out on life while we endure what seems like a purposeless trial, but when we submit prayerfully to God who is sovereign, God works that trial for our good. What is the good that God is doing in our lives?

Paul continues in verse 29, "For those whom He foreknew, He also predestined to become conformed to the image of His Son. . ." We are being molded through our trials into the image of Jesus Christ which is the process of sanctification. My family is in the process of being molded into Christ's image as we look to Him for wisdom, guidance, and strength. Trustingly, step-by-step, we walk forward through the pain and suffering with our eyes on God knowing that He is in control every moment. To keep our eyes on Him, we read His Word daily, and we hand over our circumstances to our sovereign God through prayer. When we see His provision, we praise Him and thank Him.

Michael W. Smith's song, "Sovereign Over Us," describes God's sovereignty during trials:

> There is strength within the sorrow
> There is beauty in our tears
> And You meet us in our mourning
> With a love that casts out fear
> You are working in our waiting
> You're sanctifying us
> When beyond our understanding
> You're teaching us to trust
> Your plans are still to prosper
> You have not forgotten us
> You're with us in the fire and the flood
> You're faithful forever
> Perfect in love
> You are sovereign over us[1]

God is working in our waiting. I know that His perspective is much greater than mine. Isaiah 55:9 states:

"For as the heavens are higher than the earth, So are My ways higher than your ways And My thoughts than your thoughts."

I can only see the pain and what is happening right now while God sees what we need and how He can bring about our greater good. I desire comfort, but He desires sanctification. God's plan is still to prosper me; He has not forgotten us. He is faithful forever and perfect in love. He is sovereign over us.

As we wait, we hope and are confidently assured that God is using this for our good. We trust in how God is going to work and in how He is going to change us. Indeed, I am even looking forward to seeing how different and more like Christ I am going to be on the other side.

How does knowing God is sovereign provide hope for you today?

Praise Him for being sovereign.

For further study read Psalm 103.

DAY 10

Hope in God who is the Everlasting God

Isaiah 26:3-4

"The steadfast of mind You will keep in perfect peace, because he trusts in You. Trust in the Lord forever, For in God the Lord, we have an everlasting Rock."

Isaiah 40:28

"Do you not know? Have you not heard? The Everlasting God, the LORD, The Creator of the ends of the earth does not become weary or tired. His understanding is inscrutable."

God is everlasting, His promises are everlasting, His covenant with us is everlasting. His faithfulness and love are everlasting. He does not grow weary or tired. His wisdom is unfathomable. I am none of these things. Apart from God my promises are limited or broken, my faithfulness is weak, my love is tarnished with fleshly motives, I grow weary easily, and my wisdom is entirely limited. Apart from God, I am hopeless! I have hope in God who is everlasting because He invites me to experience everlasting life, His everlasting promises, faithfulness, love, wisdom, and strength. He is all of those things we are not, and He has invited you and me to participate in eternal life with Him.

In John 4, we meet a woman who is much like us. She has experienced unfulfilled promises, unfaithfulness, rejection, and is living in brokenness. Although I cannot relate to her exact experience, I can say in truth that I have experienced variations of all of those things. As this Samaritan woman is going about her normal daily activity of drawing water from the well, she encounters Jesus. He asks her a simple question, "Give me a drink." (John 4:7) From an earthly and cultural perspective, this conversation shouldn't have even happened, he being a man, and a Jew. Jews looked down on Samaritans racially and religiously, and so the woman is taken aback. She responds with a question, "How is it that you, being a Jew, ask me for a drink since I am a Samaritan woman?" Jesus, being Everlasting God, has something to offer this woman that is far greater than just a drink of water. He responds in verse 10, "If you knew the gift of God, and who it is who says to you, 'Give me a drink.' You would have asked Him, and He would have given you living water." The woman continues to think in earthly terms and is confused because Jesus has no means to draw water from the well. Jesus replies in verse 13, "Everyone who drinks of this water will thirst again; but whoever drinks of the water that I will give him shall never thirst; but the water I will give him will become in him a well of water springing up to eternal life." The conversation continues and Jesus demonstrates that He knows the intimate details of her life. He has seen and understands her need, and is ready to fill that need for relationship, healing, and salvation. Eternal life.

Only an Everlasting God can offer us eternal life. What is eternal life? A little later in John 17:3, Jesus explains clearly what eternal life is. "This is eternal life, that they may know You, the only true God, and Jesus Christ whom You have sent." Relationship. To be in relationship with the only true God and Jesus Christ. God invites us to be in relationship with Him, to experience all of Him, His nature, eternal perspective and wisdom. As we continue to grow closer to Him, He reveals who He is, His nature, and that He is worthy of our trust. We can place our trust and hope for our future, and wisdom for today, in our everlasting God!

How does knowing God is everlasting God provide hope for you today?

Praise Him for being our Everlasting God, and inviting you to be in relationship with Him.

For further study read Psalm 90.

DAY 11

Hope in God Who is the Lord of Hosts

Ephesians 6:10

"Finally, be strong in the Lord and in the strength of His might."

There is no doubt that believers will face trials and troubles this side of heaven. Warfare is a part of the Christian life. Our opposition may come as we oppose our flesh, the world's system, or the tricky schemes of Satan. The battle may be fought on the stage of our life or the in the inner places of our hearts, yet the Lord of Hosts is able to lead us to victory! We do not have to fight our battles in our own strength.

In I Samuel 1, Hannah, a godly woman, found herself in the middle of her own intimate personal battle. Her heart hurt desperately. She was one of two wives. To make matters worse, the other woman had children while Hannah was barren. We feel her pain - the empty arms, the aching to be a mother, and the feeling of never measuring up. The doubts came in like a powerful flood. She wept and couldn't eat. She was oppressed, distressed, and in agony over the situation. The war on the inside showed on the outside.

We all face battles! Battles take place in our hearts and spring from the circumstances that surround us. When our children stray, when our marriage falls apart, when illness strikes, when our finances are depleted, when accidents take us by surprise, when loss stuns us, a battle for peace and joy is ignited in our hearts. Our outward circumstances can be extremely difficult, but the battle that wages in our hearts as a result is even tougher.

What was Hannah to do? What are we to do when we find ourselves in such a battle? Hannah called on the Lord of Hosts to provide victory for the battle that waged war in her heart. The Lord of Hosts, is also the Lord of Hope. That truth brought peace-filled victory to Hannah's heart.

Nothing had changed for Hannah, yet her sobbing turned to praise. Her anguish turned to rejoicing. God brought victory to the war-torn places of her heart.

The Lord of Hosts continually provides deliverance and victory. No battle is too big for Him to conquer. Big fear? His peace is greater! Deep hurt? There's no end to His love! Impossible circumstances? All things are possible for Him!

The Lord of Hosts is able to bring an end to any and every war-torn heart! That truth is what brought victory to Hannah's heart. She put her hope, her confident assurance, in the living God, the one that rules and reigns.

We can cease striving; we can be still and let peace reign in our hearts because God is the Lord of Hosts. Every battle we face, whether it is a battle played out in the circumstances of our life or played out in the inner places of our hearts, God is ruler over all. He is more than able to bring victory!

The words written by Martin Luther in the hymn, "A Mighty Fortress is our God," portrays the amazing hope we have in the middle of any battle we face.

"Did we our own strength confide,
Our striving would be losing,
Were not the right man on our side,
The man of God's own choosing.
Dost ask who that may be?
Christ Jesus, it is He
Lord Sabaoth (Lord of Hosts) His name,
From age to age the same,
And He must win the battle."

How does knowing that God is the Lord of Hosts give you hope today?

Praise Him for being the Lord of Hosts.

For further study, read Psalm 89: 11-18.

DAY 12

Hope in God Who Makes All Things New

Revelation 21:5

"And He who sits on the throne said, "Behold, I am making all things new." And He said, "Write, for these words are faithful and true."

Over the years, our family has spent time outdoors and have seen some very beautiful places. The views from Mt. Fuji in southern Oregon, 3-Fingered Jack, Mt. Jefferson area, and Glacier National Park in Montana are breathtaking. One of my favorite views was when I was up early at Duffy Lake. There was mist on the lake, but you could see the sun shining above it, and the sky was blue. Duffy Butte towered above the lake and looked very mysterious. It took my breath away. The earth is full of God's glory. As I saw these sights, they seemed unscarred and wildly beautiful. They remind me of heaven. Yet, we know that the earth is under tremendous strain. It is under the same curse that we are. The curse of sin. There is vast ugliness all around us. There is physical, emotional, and spiritual pain, sickness, and death. We cannot avoid it. In Revelation 21, God gives us confident assurance of a guaranteed promise. One day, everything will change.

"And I heard a loud voice from the throne, saying, "Behold, the tabernacle of God is among men, and He will dwell among them, and they shall be His people, and God Himself will be among them, and He will wipe away every tear from their eyes; and there will no longer be any death; there will no longer be any mourning, or crying, or pain; the first things have passed away." Revelation 21:3-4

God says, "Write," in Revelation 21:5. Write this down people! This is true! It is as good as already done. For those who are in chronic pain, for those who struggle with mental illness, for those facing the loss of a loved one, and for those struggling so hard with sin or because of the sin of others, this promise is like a ray of hope that penetrates the darkness. God will make all things new.

In my life there has been a thorn which has served the purpose of bringing me to my knees and causing me to understand my need for a Savior and for God's understanding. His ways are higher, and His thoughts are higher (Isaiah 55). God has given me His understanding which softens the pain and gives hope for healing, but what gives me the most hope is that one day that thorn will be gone. Wholeness will replace the brokenness. The struggle will be done.

The same is true for you! No matter the struggle, the constant ache of body or heart, One day the struggle will be over; God will make all things new!

This quote from John Piper beautifully describes what will occur for those whose faith is in Christ Jesus as Lord: "When God makes all things new, he will make us spiritually and morally as pure as flawless crystal, he will give us a body like the body of his glory, he will renovate all creation to take all futility and evil and pain out of it, and finally he himself will come to us and let us see his face. And so forever and ever we will live with pure hearts and glorious bodies on a new earth in the presence and the glory of our heavenly Father." (Sermon: Behold, I Make All Things New)

How does knowing that God will make all things new provide hope for you today?

Praise Him for His glorious plan.

For further study, read Revelation 21

DAY 13

Hope in God Who Promises to be My Keeper

Psalm 121: 5-6

"The Lord is your keeper, the Lord is your shade on your right hand. The sun shall not strike you by day, nor the moon by night."

It was right in the middle of a very hot spell in July which was unusual for the typical mild climate of the Northwest. Sweltering under the heat of the midafternoon sun, my three year old grandson insisted we find refuge in the kiddie pool in the back yard. That six inch deep, three foot wide pool didn't provide the relief we were seeking. The relief came when we situated the large yard umbrella to cast its shade right over our little swimming hole.

The circumstances of life can turn up the heat! We seek splashes of refreshment and escape, but reality has a relentless way of beating down on us. The tough stuff; the painful relationships, the upheaval of life, the collapse of our financial security, the disappointments and discouragement that beat down on us tempt us to look for relief in "the kiddie pool". When you dip your toes, the initial refreshment feels good. Distracted from the blaring heat by the splash of a "quick fix" such as that new purchase, the thrill of a new relationship, the nod of a supervisor acknowledging your hard work all sprinkle drops of refreshment that evaporate.

All while God offers us shade and protection from the glaring heat of our lives. Shade is provided for us by our very own keeper. Five times in the eight verses of Psalm 121 God reiterates His promise to be "our keeper".

A keeper is one who guards another, watches over another and, attends to another with great personal care. The Lord Himself, the most powerful, all knowing, loving God, has promised that He would be your keeper. He himself will personally watch over every detail of your life. He will protect you and be your guard!

That help you need? He knows all about it. He is there to provide it in the perfect way! No quick fixes that won't hold. He will bring help that lasts!

Does it feel as though the ground under your feet is slipping? As your keeper, God promises he will not allow your foot to be moved. He will be your firm foundation. Even if the earth quakes and the mountains move He will hold firm! His loving kindness is sure. (Isaiah 54:10)

Is there trouble all around? Your keeper knows all about the struggles you face. He will protect you.

Are you tempted to take short cuts and to give in to sinful desires? He knows, and He has provided His Spirit to lead you and guide you in the way that you should go. He sent His Son to die for you so that you could have victory over ever sin. He is the keeper of your soul!

Your keeper never takes his eye off of you! He never takes a break. He will never be caught sleeping on the job. There is never a moment or a situation that He is not fully aware. He is always ready to keep you from falling!

He has promised so much more than a little sprinkle of refreshment. He has promised that He Himself would be your keeper. That He would be your shade, protecting you, helping you, guarding and guiding you.

The fact that God is your keeper is a guarantee and offers so more than wishful thinking. You can place your hope, your confident assurance, in that guarantee and you will never be disappointed!

How does knowing that God has promised to be your keeper give you hope today?

Praise Him for His promise to be your keeper.

For further study read Isaiah 41:13-20.

DAY 14

Hope in the God Who Promises to Strengthen Me and Enable Me

Philippians 4:13

"I can do all things through Christ who strengthens me."

Feeling overwhelmed by the task before you? Think you are under qualified, and ill prepared? You are in good company. Moses, Jeremiah, Gideon, and Paul felt the same way! Moses questioned God's decision to choose him to bring the children of Israel out of Egypt. Jeremiah reminded God that he was young and didn't know what to say. Paul readily admitted he didn't have any fancy words to share. Gideon was hiding from the very people God called him to battle against.

Each of these men felt overwhelmed by the God-sized task before them. Awareness of their own limitations left them feeling fearful and inadequate. Yet, God had called them not because of their own abilities, wisdom, or talents. They could have hope no matter how overwhelming the task was that laid in front of them. They could confidently expect that God would give them the wisdom, strength, and power suitable for the size of the task He had laid before them. He had promised to be their strength and that He would enable them!

Consider that overwhelming job ahead of you. You know, that one that keeps you up at night, and paralyzes you during the day. God didn't set that task before you because you are capable. He gave it to you because *He* is capable and will work through you! He has promised that He would strengthen you and help you.

In fact, there is absolutely nothing in your life that is too difficult for God. Putting your confident expectation in God and His promise to strengthen you gives you great freedom to stop trying to fix it, manage it, or accomplish it on your own.

The sooner you admit you are not able on our own, the better! God never asked you or expected you to accomplish anything in your own strength or as a result of your own ingenuity or clever planning.

Lay aside your fear and inadequacies and place your hope in God's promise to strengthen you and empower you. Paul powerfully encourages us to hope in God's strength and not our own in 1 Corinthians 1:26-29.

"For consider your calling, brothers: not many of you were wise according to worldly standards, not many were powerful, not many were of noble birth. But God chose what is foolish in the world to shame the wise; God chose what is weak in the world to shame the strong; God chose what is low and despised in the world, even things that are not, to bring to nothing things that are, so that no human being might boast in the presence of God."

Giving up relying on ourselves and fully trusting God to strengthen and enable us for what He has called us to do allows great opportunity to bring glory to His name. God didn't choose you for the task He assigned you because you are wise, powerful, or somebody special. He assigned the task ahead to you so that His strength could be on display!

David, a shepherd boy called to be the king of Israel, spoke from experience in Psalm 31:24 when he said, "Be of good courage, And He shall strengthen your heart, All you who hope in the Lord".

The living God will strengthen and empower you for the good work He has prepared for you.

How does knowing God will strengthen and empower you give you hope today?

Praise Him for strengthening and empowering you for the work He has called you to.

For further study, read Jeremiah 1:5-8, Judges 6:11-18, and Exodus 3:10-12.

DAY 15

Hope in My Unchanging God

Malachi 3:6

"For I the Lord do not change; therefore you, O children of Jacob, are not consumed."

Change. There is no escaping the fact that change describes our existence and the world around us. The one constant we can rely on is that things change. According to God's word, we can also count on the fact that God does not change! When does that truth impact us the most? When circumstances change around us and trials occur. When we realize we don't have control over our situation or our life, we need the truth that God is unchanging, that we can count on Him to be the same. When in your life has the truth that God doesn't change impacted you? God declares about Himself that He is unchanging, and that His love and goodness never change. When we place our trust in Him, we have hope in our God that does not change.

Mark 4:35-41 describes a moment when circumstances changed very quickly. Jesus had been teaching a crowd by the Sea of Galilee. That evening Jesus said to His disciples, "Let us go over to the other side." While they were headed to the other side, a storm came up. "And there arose a fierce gale of wind, and the waves were breaking over the boat so much that the boat was already filling up." Have you ever been chugging along in life, and a storm breaks out? Life circumstances can change on a dime. We can count on that. So, what happens when change comes? When trials come, what are we to do? When the storm broke out on the lake, the disciples were very concerned. They feared for their lives. What did they do? They looked to Jesus, who was sleeping! Who sleeps in the middle of a storm? The disciples asked the same question, "Teacher, do You not care that we are perishing?" The disciples were certain that this was it! Their time was up. Their mind was set. Don't you care? How many times have we cried out to God, "Do you see what is happening here?"

"And He got up and rebuked the wind and said to the sea, 'Hush, be still.' And the wind died down and it became perfectly calm."

I can picture the disciples faces and hear their thoughts. "What just happened?" "Did you see that?" "It was storming a second ago, right?" "Those waves were going to take us over!" Yet Jesus, with His words, made it all stop. He turned to them and asked, "Why are you afraid? Do you still have no faith?" What was Jesus really asking? Was He asking if they had faith enough to stop the storm themselves, or was He asking if they were afraid He had lost control in the midst of the storm?

The disciples were overwhelmed by their circumstances, yet the Savior had not lost control. He was still in control of His very own creation. This is true for us as well. It's in those moments of chaos, those out of control broken moments when we are tempted to wonder if for a moment God has lost control. There are countless accounts of God's character on display in His word. Countless accounts of God's faithfulness, His love, His intervention in the midst of chaos. The greatest of this is the cross. He said He would do it, and He was good on His promise. God's word declares it is so, so let us not be consumed, but let us put our trust in our God who does not change.

How does knowing God doesn't change provide hope for you today?

Praise Him for being our unchanging God.

For further study, read Psalm 18:1-2, 30-36.

DAY 16 | Hope in the God of Power and Might

Jeremiah 32:27

"Behold, I am the LORD, the God of all flesh; is anything too difficult for Me?"

It is easy to underestimate God in light of our overwhelming circumstances. Captivated by the severity of our difficulties, we forget the power and might of God. The true story of Jehosephat, one of Judah's godly kings, appears in 2 Chronicles 20. He found himself surrounded by not just one enemy army, but three. Talk about overwhelming circumstances. Understandably, he was afraid.

As you look at your circumstances, perhaps you are afraid as well. If it's not one thing, it's another, and it all seems impossible!

Jehosephat recognized he was powerless. He didn't have the man-power or the resources to overtake and subdue three armies at once. There was nothing he could do. He acknowledged his own inability. Instead of panic, he looked to the Lord, and boldly acknowledged that power and might were in God's hands and nothing was too difficult for Him!

At times we fail to recognize that we cannot handle the difficulties that surround us. We go to work, trying hard to fix things and manage the messes of our lives! How much more effective it would be if we, like Jehosephat, quickly recognized that we can't do it! It is too much for us. The burden is too heavy, too complicated, and too impossible. Instead of striving, juggling, and controlling, we, too, can turn to the Lord, the God of power and might. That heavy burden, that tangled mess, that overpowering enemy, is not too much for Him. He is the God of power and might! Nothing is too difficult for Him!

Jehosephat admitted he wasn't able. There were enemies positioned against him on every side. Yet he went from being filled with fear to having confident assurance! How could that be?

Nothing had changed. The answer wasn't in a brilliant military strategy. He had genuine hope because he trusted in the God of power and might! He took his eyes off the size and magnitude of his trouble, quit trying to fix it on his own, and focused on the power and might of His God.

He *encouraged* his people by reminding them of all the times in the past they had seen God do the impossible. He *exhorted* them to pray. He *directed* them to look to the Lord, and he *reminded* them that God would be with them.

Perhaps that same encouragement, exhortation, direction, and reminder is exactly what you need today to take you from despair to hope. Afraid? Be encouraged by the times you have seen God work in the past. Pray. Tell God all about your trouble, ask Him to bring help. Keep your eyes on the Lord, remember who He is, reminding yourself of His power and might. Trust that He is with you.

With one final shout, Jehosephat told his men to believe in the Lord their God, the God of power and might. Before they could lift a hand in battle, the Lord intervened! He caused the three armies to wage war against one another. The result? The armies killed off one another, down to every last one! Complete victory for King Jehosephat and the entire nation of Judah! They hadn't lifted a hand, let alone a weapon. They only lifted their heads to look to their God!

That same God is your God! Nothing is too difficult for Him, not even the circumstances of your life. The living God is still powerful and mighty. There's no need to be afraid!

How does knowing that the living God is powerful and mighty provide hope for you today?

Praise Him for being powerful and mighty.

For further study, read I Chronicles 16:1-34.

DAY 17

Hope in the God Who Creates

Psalm 139:13

"For you formed my inward parts; You wove me in my mother's womb."

Have you ever looked at the night sky and wondered in awe at the vastness of the universe? Our galaxy alone boasts an estimated one hundred billion stars. Multiplied by the several hundred thousand million known galaxies, the number of stars roughly totals 10,000,000,000,000,000,000,000,000 or 10^{25}. Such massive figures surpass our comprehension. Certainly only God knows the exact number of stars. Contemplating just this one detail of creation, we begin to appreciate its immensity, its complexity. Only God could have done this!

Just as we marvel at the universe, with similar effort we grapple with and try to answer the big questions of life. "How did everything around us come into being?" "Why are we here?" Apart from God, man in his quest for answers offers only opinion at the expense of truth. But how can such principles of creation be understood apart from the only One whose opinion matters—the One who formed it all? Elohim, the creator God, through Scripture's account of creation answers those tough who, how, what, and why questions.

Fittingly, God first introduces Himself to man in Genesis 1:1 as Elohim, the beginning of all things. Scripture further emphasizes what we learn from creation - God's supremacy over and distinction from man. We, like the Psalmist, might ask, "When I consider Your heavens, the work of Your fingers, the moon and the stars which You have ordained; what is man that You take thought of him, and the son of man that You care for him?" (Psalm 8:3-4). The very fact that God created us reveals our significance, our worth to Him. Furthermore, what profound truth that the Maker of the countless stars, the One who holds the answer to every difficult question, Mighty Creator Elohim, wants to be known by us!

In Genesis 1:1, the beginning of the epic story of all time, we are introduced to the protagonist Elohim—"God" in our Bibles. Yet to call Him a mere character in a story is to miss the fullness of Who He is. He is the Author, the all-powerful Creator, the Designer, Master, Savior, the God of gods, the Beginning and the End, and indeed much more!

And God, the one who creates, also created YOU—personally, purposely, uniquely, and intricately. You are an original design, never to be duplicated! It is easy to be discouraged about our bodies, the way we look, our talents and abilities, and even our purpose in life. But God is our designer. Our hope is in the God who creates and formed it all. Reflect on this truth and examine God's very personal creation of each human being in Psalm 139:13-16 (below). As you read, consider the meaning of key words provided in parentheses.

"For You formed (to form, create, as a master potter) my inward parts; You wove (to weave, interweave, weave together) me in my mother's womb. I will give thanks to You, for I am fearfully (in a wonderful manner; to cause astonishment and awe) and wonderfully (to become distinguished, admirable, separate from, marked out) made; Wonderful (beyond one's power, difficult to do or understand, extraordinary) are Your works, and my soul knows it very well. My frame (bones) was not hidden from You, when I was made in secret (covering, shelter, hiding place, place of protection), and skillfully wrought (to adorn with colors, variegate, as with needlework or embroidery) in the depths of the earth; Your eyes have seen (to see, look at, perceive, inspect, consider; regard, look after, learn about, observe, watch, look upon; give attention to, gaze at; behold) my unformed substance; and in Your book were all written the days that were ordained (to form in the mind, plan, devise; to be predestined) for me, when as yet there was not one of them." (Definitions adapted from Strong's Concordance and Gesenius's Lexicon.)

How does knowing God created you provide hope for you today?

Praise Him for being the God who creates.

For further study, read Genesis 1:1- 11.

Hope in the God Who Sees

Psalm 40:11

"You, O Lord, will not withhold your compassion from me; your lovingkindness and your truth will continually preserve me."

Rejection stings! Neglect hurts! Before long, you find yourself wondering if you are invisible or worse yet, forgotten. Hagar knew all too well what it felt like to be rejected and neglected. Her story is told in Genesis 16. Hagar couldn't help but think that no one saw her pitiful life. Through no fault of her own she found herself in the middle of an unbearable situation. After years of waiting for God to fulfill His promise to give them a son, Sarah and Abraham choose to take matters into their own hands. They nominated Hagar to provide the son God had promised to them. Abraham slept with Hagar, he and Sarah's maid servant, and sure enough, she became pregnant. Despite the fact that this plan was cooked up by Sarah herself, it wasn't long before Sarah despised Hagar and made life miserable for her. Sarah treated Hagar harshly. Enduring as much abuse as she could bare, Hagar ran to a desolate place where she was out of sight, all alone, and sweltering under the desert sun. She found herself discouraged, desperate, and convinced that she had been forgotten, not just by people, but by God Himself.

Have life's blows left you feeling invisible or forgotten? Does it feel as though you have been abandoned? Have people treated you harshly? If so, you know how Hagar felt.

However, the story doesn't end there. The Lord found Hagar. (Genesis 16:7). Never for an instant had she been out of His sight. He knew all about her trouble. She had never been invisible or forgotten by Him. So convinced of this, Hagar called the Lord "El Roi", meaning "the God who sees". She went on to declare, "Truly here I have seen him who looks after me." (Genesis 16:13) Not only was she always in plain view, He had always cared for and looked after her.

No matter how invisible you feel or how much you feel forgotten by others, you can have hope, that confident assurance that God sees you right where you are. He knows all about your trouble, and He will look after you. You never have been, nor never will ever be, forgotten! The living God sees you and is looking after you!

Hagar returned to her difficult circumstances. She gave birth to her son. Life was still difficult. Sarah still couldn't stand having Hagar in her presence. Once again Hagar found herself being cast out by the people around her. Abraham packed bread and water for Hagar and sent her on her way. Once again Hagar felt abandoned by people and by God. Once again God showed up! He quickly and clearly reminded her that she was not alone. Not only did He see her, but He heard her cries as well!

Sometimes life is difficult. There is no escaping the troubles that we face, and have to endure. The hope-giving reality is that no matter how hard, no matter how long, no matter how difficult, we are never out of God's sight. He always sees us, cares for us, and looks after us. He always hears and answers us when we cry out to Him.

We always have hope because God sees and hears us! His loving, watchful eye is always on us, and His listening ear is always inclined toward us.

How does knowing God sees, hears, and is caring for you provide hope for you today?

Praise Him for being a God who sees and hears you.

For further study, read Psalm 32:7-8.

DAY 19

Hope in the Living God

Psalm 27:1

"The Lord is my light and my salvation; Whom shall I fear? The Lord is the defense of my life; Whom shall I dread ? Though a host encamp against me, My heart will not fear; though war arise against me, In spite of this I shall be confident."

David had placed His confidence in the Living God. He was absolutely sure of God and His character. No matter what troubles he encountered, David did not fear. His hope was securely anchored in the character of the Living God.

It is possible that we, unlike David, have put our faith in a god of our own making, not the Living God. It is possible that our view of God is askew. Consequently we won't trust Him. We are afraid that we will be disappointed and then doubt His goodness if the god of our making fails us! When troubles come, we live in fear.

When we paint the portrait and determine the character of our god, we are never able to trust Him. Perhaps the God we have created is much like **Santa Claus.** We view Him as a God who exists to make us happy, to give us fun and special gifts. He requires nothing in return except a little good behavior.

We may see Him as **The Rewarder.** We expect that if we serve Him and live for Him, in return He should reward us with a good life - life according to our own definition of good.

Maybe we work alongside God as if He was our **Co-Pilot.** We want God to be nearby in case we get into trouble. His job is to be on standby. He is there to comfort and support us when we need it, but He is never really in control.

At the opposite end of the spectrum, we might make him out to be a **Stern God.** We understand Him to be harsh, unforgiving, and unapproachable. Consequently, we live in fear of Him.

Some suspect that God exists to make us comfortable. He is available to ease our pain and satisfy our desires, painting Him to look much liked a Pez Candy dispenser. Present to satisfy our sweet desires. If we have created a god of our own making, when troubles come, we will doubt the goodness of God! We will be disappointed because He won't act like we expected Him too.

In my early twenties, my mom died of cancer. It rocked my world. The worst part was I found myself disappointed with God. He wasn't who I thought He was. He didn't act how I thought He should. The God I had made up would never have let mom die. She had loved Him and served Him her whole life. Surely the **"The Rewarder"** god I had envisioned would have, in return, given her a long healthy pain-free life. *I see now what I didn't see then. I had made up my own version of God.*

Yet even as I called out to Him in my heart-break, in my disappointment I discovered the Living God! A God who didn't give us what we genuinely deserve. The Living God didn't always make me comfortable but always comforted. He didn't always take away the pain but walked with me through it.

Are you disappointed with God? Do you doubt His goodness? Do you find it difficult to trust Him? Perhaps you are looking to a god of your own making.

The Living God is the God David clung to. As he clung to the living God, he concluded, "I don't have to be fearful, I don't have to doubt." In fact, he found the opposite to be true. He placed His confident assurance in the character of the Living God. He lived with hope.

How does trusting the Living God provide hope for you today?

Praise Him for being the Living True God.

For further study, read Psalm 27.

DAY 20

Hope in The Lord My Banner

Exodus 17:15

"Moses built an altar and named it The LORD is My Banner;"

⚓ In May 1940, the German army captured France and caused the retreat of nearly 400,000 Allied soldiers to Dunkirk, a small French City along the English Channel. The destruction of nearby ports prevented Allied ships from rescuing the trapped soldiers. Just fifteen miles separated them from German tanks intent on their extermination; it looked like certain death.

Winston Churchill believed that the survival of even 20,000 soldiers would be a miracle. In desperation, King George declared May 26, 1940, a national day of prayer. Entering Westminster Cathedral, Parliament, the Prime Minister, and the King lay prostrate before the Lord crying out to Almighty God for hope and deliverance.

Unknowingly cooperating with Divine sovereignty, Hitler, victory in hand, rejected the advice of his generals and illogically withdrew the German tanks' advancement on Dunkirk. Instead he ordered the German Air Force to defeat the stranded soldiers.

The very next day a dense fog suddenly rolled across the water and covered the entire English Channel. It was not the season for fog; never in recorded history had fog covered the channel in May. Obscured from the German Air Force under this heavy fog, 600 small boats traveled back and forth across the channel for several days, transporting troops to safety. As a result, 338,000 soldiers were saved. Churchill hailed this event a miracle of deliverance, proclaiming, "A guiding hand interfered to make sure the allied forces were not annihilated at Dunkirk."

It was not the size of England's army that protected her in World War II. England did not rally around her own superior strategy, bravery, or persistence. Having nowhere else to turn, she recognized her only hope was in the sovereign hand of God. Responding to the prayer of faith, the petition for His deliverance, God revealed Himself to England as Jehovah Nissi, the Lord My Banner.

In Exodus 17, the children of Israel were as desperate as the soldiers at Dunkirk and found themselves in a similarly hopeless predicament. The Amalekites' strong armies were in a battle with God's people. Moses stood on the top of a hill with the staff of God and whenever he held his staff up in the posture of godly dependence, God's people began winning the battle. When Moses lowered his hand, the Amalekites would begin winning the battle. After Amalek's defeat at Rephidim, Moses names his commemorative alter Jehohvah Nissi, The Lord is my Banner, giving full credit and glory to God for victory.

We may not be facing military battles like those of England and God's people, however, we all face daily battles as we live this life. In fact, this life on earth is a battle zone. The Bible tells us that our lives will have trials and suffering. In these trials, it is tempting to put our hope, our confident assurance, in what is horizontally in front of us. We can easily put our hope in people, money, earthly wisdom, or even our own feelings. But just like with Moses, when he tired of holding up the staff and relying on the LORD, the battle was a losing one. Without Jehovah Nissi fighting for us, victory is impossible. We need to put our hope in what is vertical; the Living God.

What is your banner? Where are you putting your hope? Where are you putting your trust, seeking fulfillment, and giving credit for your successes? Give full credit and glory to the living God by putting it in the One that you can trust and that will never let you down.

How does knowing God's role in our battles provide hope for you today?

Praise Him for being the Lord My Banner.

For further study, read Ephesians 6:10-18.

DAY 21

Hope in the Lord Our Healer

Exodus 15:26

"...for I, the Lord, am your healer."

To be honest, when I am experiencing sickness and pain, I get discouraged. I have a hard time placing my hope in the Living God. My hope is dependent on ME feeling MY best. My joy comes from my body working and my ability to do all the things I want. My peace comes from knowing I can do what I need to accomplish that day. And my security comes from my ability to make that happen. When my body fails me I get discouraged and feel hopelessness similar to God's people wandering in the desert.

The people of Israel spent many years under great oppression. From sunrise to sunset, they labored hard in the hot sun making bricks for the Egyptians in the field. It was rigorous work. The pharaohs instructed taskmasters to be ruthless; beatings and whippings occurred on a regular basis. The Israelites were in great need of a savior; a savior who could heal them physically, spiritually, and emotionally. God provided Moses to champion the redemption of the people from slavery, but Pharaoh was not willing to let them go. They watched as God sent many plagues to sway the heart and intentions of Pharaoh, but his heart remained hardened. The Egyptians suffered plague after plague. It was not until after God took the firstborn son of every family which did not follow the Passover that He provided the timing and protection for Moses to lead them away from slavery to freedom and the Promised Land.

Beyond the Exodus and through the miraculous crossing of the Red Sea, the children of Israel find themselves in the middle of the desert with only bitter water. Three days later they were tired and thirsty, their physical bodies were withering from the heat.

Naming the place Marah, meaning bitter, because they believed the Lord had dealt bitterly with them. Did they remember the God who had just rescued them from captivity by parting a sea of water? Did they really believe that God, who had just saved their lives, would now allow them to die?

God brought His people to this place to test them and teach them obedience. He also revealed to them that He is the Lord our healer (Exodus 15:26). Only seven miles from Marah was Elim where there were twelve springs of water and seventy palm trees which provided the people with healing through water and shade. The LORD, however, did not take the people there first. He wanted the opportunity to first expose their heart. Out of the heart of the Israelites came grumbling and discouragement.

When we are obedient and walking faithfully with the LORD, He blesses us even in our suffering. These blessings are not always seen when we encounter situations like the bitter waters of Marah. Life difficulties are not what we would expect to receive. God will not always lead us straight to Elim with water and shade. However He will always use the bitter waters we encounter and make them sweet in His time. We can rest knowing that He will restore what was once broken. God uses our sickness, pain, and suffering to expose what is in our heart. What comes out of our hearts when we don't feel our best or are in pain? Is it discouragement, grumbling, worry, anxiety, hopelessness, and depression? Our heart shows us where we are finding our hope, joy, peace, and security. Instead of finding it in the way we feel, look to the LORD our healer for He IS our hope. Because He himself has suffered, He promises that He will help those who are suffering!

How does knowing God's role in our healing provide hope for you today?

Praise Him for being the Lord My Healer.

For further study, read Hebrews 2:10-18.

DAY 22

Hope in the Lord Who is My Peace

John 14:27

"Peace I leave with you; My peace I give to you; not as the world gives do I give to you. Do not let your heart be troubled, nor let it be fearful."

Yesterday I saw a surgeon regarding abdominal pain and left his office with two appointments: one for a nuclear medicine scan and one for a diagnostic procedure. I don't know what is going to be discovered, and, honestly, my attitude after the appointment was irritated, fearful, apprehensive, and annoyed that this problem has presented itself in my life. I felt that I have better things to do with my time and energy than to walk down the path of medical diagnosis and possibly surgery. Behind that annoyance, really, is fear.

Jesus knows that our hearts become troubled and fearful by the various circumstances in our lives. Even when my life is going well, I am afraid of when the next trial might come my way. Life often changes in a moment. Jesus, who knows all things, begins in John 14:1 with, "Do not let your heart be troubled; believe in God, believe also in Me." Our faith in God and His Son, Jesus, keeps us from being troubled. Why is that? Is it wishful thinking?

Jesus stated in John 14:27, "Peace I leave with you; My peace I give to you; not as the world gives do I give to you. Do not let your heart be troubled, nor let it be fearful." God is the source of our peace, but Jesus is more specific than that. In verse 26, the verse before, he stated, "But the Helper, the Holy Spirit, whom the Father will send in my name, He will teach you all things, and bring to your remembrance all that I said to you." Jesus does not give as the world gives. The world offers us false security in people, money, knowledge, and physical things that fail us. When we encounter trials, we may turn to our friends, the internet, alcohol, drugs, food, or money. The world does not help us, fulfill us, or solve our problems. Jesus gives us something different; He gives us Himself in the form of the Holy Spirit. The Spirit is called the Helper. He abides with us, teaches us, and brings to remembrance the words of Jesus. He is the peace that Jesus leaves with us. With the Holy Spirit, we do not need to let our hearts be troubled or fearful. No matter what we face, Jesus Himself is with us.

Our faith is also in God's character. His character includes His sovereignty and His omniscience. God's sovereignty means that He is in control of all things; God's omniscience means that He knows all things. In the case of my medical situation, God knows what is causing my pain. He is not surprised by it and has a plan for how He is going to use it to sanctify me, mold me further into the image of Jesus. God, who is my peace, is sovereign and in control of my health. Nothing will happen to me that has not passed through His hands, and as it passes through His hands, He uses it to make me more like His Son, Jesus.

No matter what happens in my life, I am not alone. The God who created this world, who controls the sun, moon, stars, and seas, the God who knows the number of hairs on my head and the name of every celestial body, is with me through His Spirit. He is my peace because He gives me wisdom when I ask for it, because He perfectly provides for me, and because He is in control of every circumstance in my life. While I go through each day, I have hope, confident assurance, in God who is my peace. That peace is His presence.

_____

How does knowing God is our peace provide hope for you today?

Praise Him for being your peace.

For further study, read John 14.

DAY 23

Hope in the Lord Who Sanctifies

1 Corinthians 6:11
"Such were some of you; but you were washed, but you were sanctified, but you were justified in the name of the Lord Jesus Christ and in the Spirit of our God."

Ever since Adam ate of the forbidden fruit in the Garden of Eden, every person has been born with a sin nature. This means that our natural propensity is to sin. Sin is everything you think, say, or do that is wrong and against God's commands. This means that every one of us sins, has a sin nature, and is in need of forgiveness of sins and sanctification, which means to be set apart for God and to be holy. We cannot accomplish this on our own, but we have hope, confident assurance, that our God is the Lord who sanctifies.

How does God sanctify us? Something that is sanctified cannot be tainted by sin because it is set apart from sin for God. Since we have sin natures, we are tainted by sin. Sin has a price that we cannot pay. "For the wages of sin is death, but the free gift of God is eternal life in Christ Jesus our Lord." (Romans 6:23) In His great love for us (John 3:16), He sent Jesus Christ, His Son, to earth as a man to die on the cross to pay the price for our sin. He died, was buried, and rose again on the third day. He ascended to heaven and is currently seated at God's right hand. He is praying and interceding for us as we speak.

Our sin is paid for, forgiven, and we are free, but we still live with the presence of sin until Jesus returns to restore all of creation. The good news is that when we believe that Jesus died, was buried, and rose again for our salvation from sin, God seals us with His Holy Spirit as a promise of our eternal salvation (Ephesians 1:13). His Holy Spirit is at work in us every day sanctifying us which means He is changing us and molding us to be set apart from sin. He is daily making us into the image of His Son, Jesus Christ.

What does it look like to be sanctified daily? We know that the trials and difficulties we experience here on earth are not wasted. Romans 8:28-30 states, "And we know that God causes all things to work together for good to those who love God, to those who are called according to his purpose. For those whom he foreknew, He also predestined to become conformed to the image of His Son, so that He would be the first born among many brethren; and these whom He predestined, He also called; and these whom He called, He also justified; and these whom He justified, He also glorified." God works all things to mold us who belong to Him into the image of His Son Jesus. This is the process of sanctification. Jesus went through the same process when He was on earth. Hebrews 5:8 says, "Although He was a Son, He learned obedience from the things which He suffered." As I suffer, I can also learn obedience like Christ did. I can lean into God and His Word and chose obedience and sanctification.

We know that when we believe in Christ, God is sanctifying us through His Holy Spirit and His Word. We are promised the completion of this process in Philippians 1:6, "For I am confident of this very thing, that He who began a good work in you will perfect it until the day of Christ Jesus." This is His work in me that He will complete. I have hope, confident assurance, that while I am currently in the process of sanctification, one day I will stand fully sanctified before God.

How does knowing God who sanctifies us provide hope for you today?

Praise Him for sanctifying us.

For further study, read Romans 8.

DAY 24

Hope in God Who is Near to the Broken Hearted

Psalm 34:18
"The Lord is near to the brokenhearted and saves the crushed in spirit."

It was his first crush. The bubbly brunette who I had seen flirt with my middle school aged son. It all seemed fun and innocent. Cute even. Until she moved on, like most girls her age do. I knew it was inevitable. I tried to prepare him. Yet the sting of rejection always hurts, even an awkward middle school boy.

I walked into his room one morning, greeted with dirty socks, mounds of clothes and sports paraphernalia strung all over. Buried in the clutter was his open Bible, with Psalm 34:18 underlined. "The Lord is near to the brokenhearted and saves the crushed in spirit."

My momma's heart swelled with acknowledgement of how powerful God's Word is to meet us in our hurt. Even the hurt of a young middle school boy.

I knew this was the first of many heartbreaks he would experience. Not all of them being the result of a girl. There would be deeper, different kinds of hurts; the pain that comes as a result of other's sin, the injury that takes place because he wouldn't always walk in step with the Lord. People he would pour his life into would disappoint him. The pain that is inevitable because we live in a sin fallen world.

As his mama, I wanted to protect him from all of it. I still do! No matter how much I want to, I'm not able. I can't protect him or anyone else from the blows of this world. We all are the walking wounded. We all have hurts, disappointments and pain. We try so hard to protect ourselves and others from the hurt and the pain that results, but it's impossible.

I can't offer answers, I can't heal the hurt. None of us can. Yet, we can still have hope; confident assurance in God's promise that He is near when we are hurting! So near in fact, he collects our tears in a bottle (Psalm 56:8).

When your heart is broken He is near! He stands with you. He knows the depth of your pain. He will walk with you through it. Those wounds that are so significant that you fear will never heal, that injury so great your heart is breaking, He knows all about them. He is right there with you. He never leaves you.

Not only has He promised to be with you, but He has promised to heal your broken heart. "He heals the brokenhearted and binds up their wounds" Psalm 147:3.

The Lord, the Creator of the universe, the all-powerful One, will gently bring healing to your broken heart. Like a balm for your soul, He will sooth the hurting places. He will mend back together where it has been torn in two.

There is hope for healing of your broken heart. No matter who or what inflicted the pain. Perhaps your heart hurts because of your own sin and sinful choices. God can heal that broken heart! He sent His Son to forgive you and to remove every stain that is a result of it.

Maybe your heart is broken because of the pain inflicted by another. God can heal that broken heart. You are not alone. God is with you. He will never leave you, forsake you or hurt you.

Perhaps circumstances of life have dealt their relentless blows and you feel as though you can hardly catch your breath, your heart is heavy and hurting. God can heal that broken heart. He will carry that burden for you. He will flood your aching heart with peace.

No matter the significance of the injury your heart has sustained you can count on God being the One who will heal your broken heart.

The same God who is near when a young boy's heart is hurting, is near to you! He has promised He would be!

How does knowing that God has promised to be near to the broken hearted provide hope for you today?

Praise Him for being near to the broken hearted.

For further study, read Psalm 34:15-22, 147:1-6.

DAY 25

Hope in Lord, Jehovah

Exodus 3:14
"God said to Moses, 'I AM WHO I AM,' and He said, 'Thus you shall say to the sons of Israel, 'I AM has sent me to you.'"

I was looking forward to a great birthday! I had plans to meet my girlfriend for coffee and crepes, followed by shopping and pedicures. Dinner was going to be equally fabulous. My husband was going to be taking me out to the new restaurant in town. I was especially intrigued by the obvious excitement he had over a gift he had bought me. Yes! It was going to be a wonderful day!

I jumped out of bed and headed down to the laundry room to get my favorite blouse. Six feet from the door the floor under my toes was sopping wet. Oh no! Apparently, the late night load of laundry did not go well. The laundry room and half the hallway were soaked. I quickly cancelled my plans for breakfast with my friend. I was stuck at home waiting for the repair man. At least I still had dinner to look forward to!

By late afternoon, life was back on track. Excited, I showered and got dressed, and waited. "Where is he?" I wondered. Finally the phone rang. "I am so sorry, Hon, I am stuck here at work in an emergency last minute meeting. Can I make it up to you tomorrow?" My heart sunk. This day had turned out nothing like what I had anticipated.

It has been said: "Blessed is he that expects nothing, for he shall never be disappointed." [1739 B. Franklin Poor Richard's Almanac (May)]. This day certainly supported that maxim.

Perhaps you feel that way too! Tough circumstances have brought disappointment. People haven't lived up to your expectations. It seems nothing you have looked forward to or anticipated has actually come to fruition.

You are not alone. No doubt Moses felt the same way. He grew up and lived as royalty in the palace of Pharaoh. He was poised for great things. Yet, life didn't turn out how he expected. Instead of prestige and prominence, he spent forty long years shepherding his father-in-law's sheep. Life was not all Moses had expected. What a disappointment!

At least it seemed that way....until God revealed Himself to Moses in Exodus 3:14 as "Yahweh," saying, "I AM WHO I AM." The very first time God refers to Himself as "Yahweh" is to Moses, a disappointed, washed up shepherd not even herding his own sheep.

Nothing could have topped the personal presence of God in Moses's life. No achievement, no possession, no degree of prominence could have been more magnificent than God personally revealing Himself in a personal way to Moses. When God told Moses that He was the "I AM," He was telling him I am real, I am unchangeable, I am self-fulfilled, and I want to be known by you.

Are you disappointed with how life has turned out? Do you feel forgotten, trapped in what seems to be menial work? Have your thoughts of how life would unfold been dashed? God is saying to you, just like He did to Moses, "I AM WHO I AM," I want to be known by you.

Let that truth settle in your heart and mind. The God and Creator of the universe wants you to know Him personally. There is hope, confident assurance for you right in the middle of the mundane and the everyday! You can know and continue to grow in your understanding and experience of the God of the Universe who personally sent His Son Jesus so that you could have a personal relationship with Him.

Knowing the God of the Universe in a personal way will trump every disappointment and every trouble and change the mundane to the magnificent.

How does knowing God is the Lord Jehovah provide hope for you today?

Praise Him for being Lord Jehovah.

For further study, read Exodus 3:1-15.

DAY 26

Hope in God Who is Love

I John 4: 16
"So we have come to know and to believe the love God has for us. God is love, and whoever abides in love abides in God and God abides in Him."

⚓ When you are hoping that someone loves you, you will act quite differently than when you are assured of their love. I am reminded of this when I think about how I acted, and what I worried about when I wanted so desperately to win over the affections of a handsome young man. Thirty-five years of marriage later I have a confidence of his unconditional love. I act differently than that insecure teenager of long ago. The same is true when we are confident of God's love for us.

God is the origin of all genuine love. Jesus told a parable to help us comprehend the love the Father has for us. He tells of a man who had a prodigal son, who insisted on receiving his inheritance early, and ran off to enjoy wanton pleasure miles away from home. When his resources were depleted and he was miserable, he returned home in hopes that his father would have mercy on him and allow him to be one of his hired servants.

When his father heard of his son's return, he welcomed him with loving arms. He went so far as to run to his son at his first glimpse of his son approaching the long road home. *The Father's love pursued!*

The father immediately wrapped his arms around his son, warmly embracing him, before he had any idea if his son was sorry or regretted his actions. *The Father's love was unconditional!*

Upon the son's arrival, the father quickly called for the best robe, a ring for his finger, and shoes for his feet. He planned a full blown celebration in honor of the son's return. *The Father poured out His love abundantly!*

God pursues us and loves us not only unconditionally, but abundantly. He is not content to love us at a distantance, but comes running toward us with open arms. He doesn't withhold His love until we are acting right. Rather, He is involved personally and powerfully, relentlessly pouring His love into our lives.

In fact, God has only love, compassion and the deepest affection for us. He has no wrath for us, whatsoever! The prodigal, upon returning home, was welcomed by a father who had only love for him. There were no dues to pay, no penitence to be made, only love to be received.

No amount of miles, no degree of foolishness or sin could separate the son from the father's love. What hope for the prodigal. What hope for each of us.

God's very character is love so we can confidently expect that all His dealings with us will flow out of His unchangeable character of love. We are simply left to live loved!

We can lived loved:
> ~Rest assured of God's unshakeable love
> (Jeremiah 31:3).
> ~Respond to His love instead of trying to earn it
> (John 3:16).
> ~Confident that nothing can separate us from His
> Love (Romans 8:39).
> ~Assured of our position in God's family (I John 3:1).
> ~Praise and thank Him for His everlasting love
> (Psalm 100:4-5).

How does knowing God is love provide hope for you today?

Praise Him for being a God of love.

For further study, read Psalm 136.

DAY 27

Hope in God Most High

Psalm 57:2
"I cry out to God Most High, to God who fulfills His purposes for me."

⚓ Dance party! The grandkids loved to sing and dance. I quickly put on Pandora Kids' Praise. It wasn't long and a song I sang as a child started playing. I had belted out the words for years but had never given them much thought. You, me, brothers, sisters, moon, stars, mommies, and babies...He's got the whole world in His hands.

As I listened and the kids danced around my feet the precious truth began to sink in. I reflected on my long life. I had learned about God over the years. Attended several Bible studies and got up early regularly to drink in God's Word.

As I listened to my grandkids sing along, I reflected on this precious truth. God reminded me that this wasn't just a cute little song and a memorable tune, but a deep theological truth that impacts all of our lives, at every level and every age. It was just as true for my four year old granddaughter as it was for me.

God did have the whole world in His hands, and each individual life. After all, one of His names is "El Elyon," meaning God Most High. And certainly He is! He is sovereign over all, all powerful, lovingly cares for His creation and is far above any other god or man.

What hope that brought to my heart. I could confidently expect God to be God, to be over all, to have the whole world in His hands, including my life and those I love. It wasn't up to me.

Mistakenly we think we are in control, orchestrating the comings and goings of our lives and others. Even taking credit for our accomplishments and success just like King Nebuchadnezzar in Daniel 4.

King Nebuchadnezzar boasted about His own accomplishments and failed to acknowledge God's hand in his success. In viewing himself as god of his own kingdom, he failed to recognize that every blessing, every success that he had experienced was a gift from the hand of God.

As a result, God humbled King Nebuchadnezzar and sent him to live among the ox. His hair grew as long as eagle feathers and his nails as long as bird claws. He lived as a recluse until the day he acknowledged God as Most High!

God is still reigning on His throne, absolutely sovereign in how He rules over all of His creation. Our lives are in His Hands!

We can be confident that every good gift is from His hand and a result of Him reigning on high.

We can also be confident that when life looks out of control and all we see is chaos, He is still reigning on high. Nothing is out of His control.

The scope of life is all under His control. From the babies to the elderly, the poor to the affluent, the sick and suffering to the strong and healthy, all has been orchestrated by His sovereign hand and He has determined what is best!

Paul understood this and was able to say, "...for I have learned in whatever situation I am to be content. I know how to be brought low, and I know how to abound. In any and every circumstance, I have learned the secret of facing plenty and hunger, abundance and need" (Philippians 4:10-13).

Paul could make such a bold proclamation because He trusted God Most High. We can trust Him too. We can put our hope and our confident assurance in Him because He is Lord Most High, reigning over every detail of our lives!

How does knowing God is Most High give you hope today?

Praise Him for being God Most High.

For further study, read Daniel 4:28-37.

DAY 28 | Hope in the Promise of Heaven

John 14:2-3

"In My Father's house are many dwelling places; if it were not so, I would have told you; for I go to prepare a place for you. If I go and prepare a place for you, I will come again and receive you to Myself, that where I am, there you may be also."

When our kids were three, five and seven we took off in an over loaded van headed to Disneyworld from Salem, Oregon. 3000 miles, thirty happy meals and one broken windshield later we arrived. The countless questions of "how much longer?" along with the endless hours were worth every minute once we arrived! For five days it truly was the happiest place on earth for our little family.

The carrot of Disneyworld helped us to hold on, sit still and endure the miles. Heaven is our carrot here on earth. Jesus promised those that believe in Him that He is preparing a place for us, and at the right time we will get to join Him there. We don't know a lot about heaven, but we do know there will be no tears, no sorrow, no pain, no darkness and no sin. We will be in the presence of our Savior and will worship Him forever. We know enough to recognize it will be worth whatever we endure during our days here on earth.

The hope, the confident assurance that one day we will be in heaven with our Savior helps us to persevere today. The bumps along the road won't seem so severe. In fact, Paul says that they will seem "light and momentary" when compared to the glories of eternity. We will recognize that the sin, trials and troubles of today will not last forever. Sin will be conquered and suffering will end. There will be no more troubles. The assurance of heaven enables us to persevere.

The hope of heaven gives us a new perspective for the here and now. The short number of days we have here on earth compared with eternity in heaven helps us recognize the futility of living our life here on earth in pursuit of things that won't last. The hope of heaven influences what we do with our time, talents and treasures. We won't want to waste our limited time here on earth on things that can provide only momentary comfort, satisfaction or recognition.

We won't place such high importance on earthly achievements that won't count for anything in heaven's economy.

The promise of heaven encourages us to value and invest in the eternal. We will more readily consider others more important than ourselves, and be concerned about their eternity when we are confident of heaven for ourselves. We won't consider this world system our home.

Hope of heaven frees us from the need to understand God's work in the here and now. We won't have to question the things that don't make sense now because we will recognize they are part of a much bigger picture that God is in the process of painting.

Confident assurance in God's promise of eternity in heaven with our Savior changes everything! That is our glorious hope.

_____

How does the promise of heaven give you hope today?

Praise Him for the promise of heaven.

For further study, read I Thessalonians 4:13-17.

DAY 29

Hope in the God Who Heals

Psalm 107:19-20
"Then they cried out to the Lord in their trouble; He saved them out of their trouble; "

Having never been out of the country before there were many sights and sounds that were foreign to me. I could get used to the trash in the road and the constant honking of motorcycles racing through the streets. Even the armed guard that stood watch over the girls at the orphanage started to seem normal. However, I would never get used to seeing the emptiness in the little girls' eyes that were new to Faith House orphanage in Jacmel, Haiti, where our team would spend ten days.

Those dark, lifeless eyes haunted me. They were a window into their souls. Souls that had been hurt deeply by unspeakable evil done to them. The depravity of man had inflicted serious injury onto those precious, vulnerable little girls. I knew the outward scars would heal, but what about their hearts? Was it even possible for joy to find its way into their lives?

I wonder if the people of Israel had similar haunting, empty eyes. They spent many years oppressed, enslaved to the Egyptians. From sunrise to sunset they labored under the hot sun. Their task masters were ruthless. Beatings and whippings occurred on a regular basis.

Could anything heal such deep hurt?

Perhaps you feel like things will never be better and that you are damaged beyond repair. Your eyes are empty and your life feels hopeless. Is there hope for you today? Is healing even possible?

Six months later I returned to Haiti, to the same orphanage, to the same little girls. There was something different. I saw evidence of God's healing power. It showed in their eyes. Where they once were empty they now sparkled with joy! There was no denying or missing that God had brought healing to these precious little ones. He had redeemed what man had meant for evil and brought good from it. He had restored their broken lives and hearts. He had brought healing to the deepest places.

They danced and sang with great enthusiasm about Jesus. The words to their favorite song ring in my thoughts daily...

"I'm not worried 'bout a thing, cause I know You are guiding me, where You lead me, Lord I will go, I have no fear 'cause I know Who's in control. There's no limit to what You can do 'cause it all belongs to You, yes, it all belongs to You. You're almighty and all powerful, and it all belongs to you, yes it all belongs to You."

It was clear God had done an amazing work of healing in their little lives.

God promised the same healing to the Israelites in Exodus 15:26, when He said, "I am the Lord, your healer." Healing that would reach far past the physical ailments and diseases to the very hearts of His people.

Surely, God heals us as well! He doesn't reserve His healing powers for just the children in orphanages and the Israelites. He is still Jehovah Rophe, the God who heals. His greatest act of healing comes as a result of Jesus' death, burial and resurrection, and is available for us today.

Sin kills, but there is a remedy! There is healing for that! We no longer have to live entrapped by sin or weighed down by the weight of sin.

We don't have to remain contaminated by the results of others sin against us. God is our Healer. We can have hope and confidence that His healing in our hearts and lives is a sure thing! _____

How does knowing that God is your healer give you hope today?

Praise Him for being a God who heals.

For further study, read Exodus 15.

DAY 30 | Hope in the God Who is Good

Psalm 25:8
"Good and upright is the Lord; therefore He instructs sinners in the way."

We all face troubles of various kinds. Oftentimes we find ourselves right smack dab in the middle of the hard. The hard that we never asked for or invited into our lives. Yet there we are; surrounded, even invaded by the trouble. We are not unique. James tells us that we all will have different kinds of trouble. Paul tells us not to be surprised that we have trouble and Jesus even acknowledged that in this world we *will* have trouble. Trouble is common, but none the less painful.

David, had trouble too! In Psalm 27 he tells us a little about his trouble. There were enemies surrounding him. Armies strategically located to attack. People had not only misunderstood him, but even his family members had deserted him. Yes! There was trouble.

Your trouble may come in a different form. Maybe your trouble has come clothed as sickness, financial difficulties, rejection, criticism; maybe you are misunderstood or mistreated.

Since we know that we will have trouble, the important question is "What do you look for in the middle of your trouble?" Honestly, I am quick to look for a solution, relief of some kind. Even retribution if someone else is the cause of my trouble. When the trouble wains on I am tempted to look for something to dull the pain.

David, however, sought something entirely different. He says "One thing have I asked of the Lord. That will I seek after; that I may dwell in the house of the Lord all the days of my life, to gaze upon the beauty of the Lord and to inquire in His temple" (Psalm 27: 4). The one thing David sought when he found himself in the middle of trouble was the Lord! Nothing else!

David understood that no matter the trouble, the severity, the length, the crushing weight, the magnificence of the Lord, the wonder of His character and His glorious beauty was far greater. It was God's character that would see him through. He wanted nothing more than to settle down in the presence of the Lord.

Even so, the trouble didn't end. There were still enemies, misunderstanding, and abandonment. David had done all the right things. He sought the Lord. He clung to His character. He settled down in His presence. Yet, trouble prevailed.

It is easy to get discouraged and lose hope when the trouble persists. David, however refused to despair. He believed He would see the goodness of God in the land of the living (Psalm 27:13). David knew that he would not only see the goodness of God in heaven, but that he would also see God's goodness "in the land of the living." In this life's arena. In the right here and right now.

Jesus didn't die just for our past and our future. He died for our "today." He died to give us hope for the tough stuff of today. His Spirit, the same Spirit that raised Christ from the dead, lives in us to give us victory, to redeem and restore relationships, to provide everything that we need for life and godliness.

He died so that we could experience His goodness today! He is good! His character is draped in goodness. He is essentially, absolutely and consummately good.

Your trouble is no match for God's goodness. You have hope! You can confidently anticipate God to be good right in the middle of it all!

_____

How does knowing God is good give you hope today?

Praise Him for being a God who is good.

For further study, read Psalm 27.

Made in the USA
San Bernardino, CA
25 November 2015